To
Denis

with fondest memories
and thanks for all the laughs!

STROLLING WITH STEAM
Walks along the Keswick Railway

Jan Darrall

Published by Sigma Leisure – an imprint of
Sigma Press, 1 South Oak Lane, Wilmslow, Cheshire SK9 6AR, England.

British Library Cataloguing in Publication Data
A CIP record for this book is available from the British Library.

ISBN: 1-85058-448-6

Typesetting and Design by: Sigma Press, Wilmslow, Cheshire.

Cover photograph: Pat Darrall

Illustrations: David Turnbull

Maps: Jan Darrall

Printed by: Manchester Free Press

Disclaimer: the information in this book is given in good faith and is believed to be correct at the time of publication. No responsibility is accepted by either the author or publisher for errors or omissions, or for any loss or injury howsoever caused. Only you can judge your own fitness, competence and experience.

Preface

This book originated from of the pleasure I experienced re-discovering the old railway line. I remember travelling on the trains to Penrith with my father before I was old enough to go to school, but since then, have not really set foot on the line for twenty years, despite living near Keswick all my life. I was very surprised therefore after discovering the delights of the line, that there was no publication linking the railway route with other footpaths in the area, and hence decided to tackle this task myself !

The walks (bar Walk 1) are all circular, and vary in length and undulation. The railway line is excellent underfoot, but walkers would be advised to wear boots or wellingtons for many of the woodland and field walks, particularly after rainy periods. The line is also fairly flat, and suitable for the disabled and elderly along most of its course.

The book begins with a brief section on the history of the line, and more specific information is also contained in the individual walks. For those interested in the historical aspects of the CKPR, I would recommend Harold Bowtell's book 'Rails Through Lakeland' (1989). The main railway route is described in Walk 1, outwards from Keswick to Threlkeld, and Keswick to Braithwaite. Each walk begins with a railway section, described in Walk 1, so as to avoid repetition. The walks can be picked up anywhere along the circular routes, and possible access points have been noted in Walk 1 and on the map at the beginning. Walks can be shortened or lengthened, or linked as required. Unfortunately, there are few walks in the Braithwaite area, as the A66 occupies much of the old route, and many of the bridges have been dismantled. Parking is available at most sites, but I have left that up to the discretion of the individual.

The National Park Authority should be complimented on the work they have done, particularly on the Keswick to Threlkeld part of the line. The display boards are excellent, but it seems a shame that there is not one at Keswick Station. It would also be nice if the original bridge number plates and names were put on the bridges (as on canal bridges).

Finally, please observe the Country Code, and respect the countryside and its inhabitants. I hope that you enjoy some or all of the walks in the book as much as I have done.

Acknowledgements

I would like to thank my family and close friends for continually supporting and encouraging me in this venture. Particular thanks are due to Mum and Dad for accompanying me on many a wet walk along the railway; to Mae and Dad for painstakingly proof-reading the text; and to David for drawing the sketches. Finally, thanks as ever to Jessie, never one to refuse a walk of any kind, whatever the place or the weather . . .

Jan Darrall

Contents

A Brief History of the CKP Line

The Cockermouth - Keswick - Penrith line (CKP) was the third railway line into the Lakes (after the Windermere and Coniston lines). It was built largely to transport iron ore from the West Cumberland mines, to the blast furnaces in the north east.

The Railway was constructed under an Act of Parliament of August 1, 1861, and the Chairman of the Company cut the first sod with an ornamental spade on May 21, 1862. Its estimated cost was £200,000. The line opened to mineral traffic on November 4, 1864, and to passengers on January 2nd, 1865. It had a total length of 31 miles, and was the highest railway in Cumbria, reaching 856 feet above sea-level at Troutbeck. The Keswick Hotel was built at a cost of £12,000, and opened in 1866/67. During the Second World War, Roedean schoolgirls were housed here. The Keswick yard moved significant amounts of goods traffic – Buttermere green slate from Honister; timber, pit props and wood, Keswick pencils, straw, sugar, and sheep for despatch to winter pastures!

A typical timetable would be the 11am train from Keswick, arriving at London Euston at 7pm. An average of 6 to 9 trains per day ran each way between Keswick and Penrith in the early 1900s, the journey taking approximately 35 minutes. During the Second World War, special trains were run for the Roedean School girls at the start and end of terms. During July every year, "Budd's Specials" were also run – special trains to carry people to and from the Keswick Convention (named after J.T. Budd who first advertised these trains). From January 1955, diesel trains were introduced to the line, some of the earliest anywhere on the British Railways line.

By 1960, the CKP line was losing £50,000 a year. The Cockermouth to Keswick section of the line was closed to passengers in April 1966. The decline and withdrawal of services on the Keswick to Penrith section began in 1966. In 1967, only five trains a day operated each way between Keswick and Penrith and, in December 1967, the track was reduced to a single line, with double track and signal boxes being taken out of use. From 1 July 1968, there were no staff at Keswick, and finally, on 6 March 1972, the line was fully closed, with the last train – a Royal Train – running on 22 April, 1972. Admirers of the route paid their respects on 4 March, a snowy cold day. Extra diesel units were put on to cater for the demand for seats. Keswick and Penrith Round Table also ran a special last trip, with 400 passengers, and Penrith town band played 'Auld Lang Syne'.

The chief reason the line disappeared was therefore because it was uneconomic. Secondly, basic traffic in coke westwards had virtually disappeared with the decline of the collieries; and thirdly, by the early 1960s, there was pressure by the Ministry of Transport to build a new road between Penrith and Workington, and the railway route provided an ideal foundation for this road. "Perhaps if the closures had been postponed only a few years, more lines would have survived, for some of the railways once feared by Wordsworth and Ruskin have come to be revered as tourist attractions in their own right" (Paul Hindle, 1989).

The Keswick to Penrith section of the line was famous, both for its beautiful views through the Greta Gorge, and for its highly individual bridge structures. In 1963, Norman Nicholson noted that the line was skilfully hidden from view, so that from above, the engine smoke seemed to issue mysteriously from fissures in the earth; and the trains looked far more at home on the fells than many human beings. Similarly, in 1933, H.H. Symonds had noted that " . . . by Threlkeld, the train was smothered under the glory of Saddleback . . . These are 6 miles of 'parly third' which leave the world's Best Permanent Way, the Royal Scot, the thunders of Shap Summit, nowhere."

As well as its scenery, the CKPR line was notable for the aesthetic and technical interest of the bridges. Through the Greta Gorge, the railway crossed the River Greta 8 times, requiring the design and creation of individual bridges, including three upright bow-string bridges, and four inverted bow-strings. The running of heavier engines in the early twentieth century required considerable re-strengthening of the bridges.

Bibliography

Bowtell, Harold D.: **Rails through Lakeland. An illustrated history of the Workington-Cockermouth-Keswick-Penrith Railway**, 1887 – 1972. Silver Link Publishing Ltd: Kettering. 1989

Hindle, Paul: 'Roads, canals and railways' in Rollinson, William (Ed): **The English Lake District, Landscape and Heritage.** David and Charles: Newton Abbot. 1989

Keswick Railway Footpath: a scenic walk through the Greta Gorge – Linda Reinecke, and Keith Davies. Ferguson Bros: Keswick. 1992

Nicholson, Norman: **Portrait of the Lakes.** Robert Hale Ltd: London. 1963

Symonds, H.H.: **Walking in the Lake District.** W & R Chambers Ltd: Edinburgh. 1933

Video – **'Trains to Keswick'**: Narrated by Alan Cartner, and produced by William Cartner. Lapwing Productions: Carlisle. 1933

Flora, Fauna, Wildlife and Geology

This section is far from detailed or exclusive, aiming to give just a few pointers to what can be seen in the area.

Flora

The ground cover along the railway line provides some colour throughout the seasons – clovers, vetches, stitchwort and brambles. In spring, bluebells, violets, stitchwort and primroses flower among the ferns, bracken and ivys. These give way not only to broom and gorse bushes, but also to wild strawberries, herb robert, foxgloves, cranesbill, bladder and red campion, enchanter's nightshade, ragwort, betony, trailing St John's wort, meadowsweet and other plants. River flora includes water crowfeet and water starwort, some of the few plants which can tolerate fast flowing water.

The most common trees are silver birch, rowan, sycamore, ash, hazelnut, hawthorn, oak and beech, with alder and willow in the wetter places. In many places, the trees form their own enclosed tunnels, beautiful in early spring and autumn. The Low Briery Bobbin mills used certain types of coppiced wood – ash, birch, sycamore, alder and lime, and past coppicing activities are still evident, where trees were cut down to just above ground level to encourage multiple trunks.

Fauna and wildlife

A range of the usual common birds can be seen while walking

Fauna and wildlife

A range of the usual common birds can be seen while walking along the railway and other more unusual birds, such as nut-hatches and tree creepers, are occasionally seen. Along the river, ducks and dippers are obvious. The River Greta is also home to fish such as Brown Trout, Sea Trout, and Salmon, and many

Shell Duck

invertebrates, including flatworms, leeches, stoneflies, mayflies and molluscs. Animals which may be observed include deer, and rabbits.

Leaping salmon

Geology

The local rocks form part of the Skiddaw Slate series, outcropping the northern Lake District. The river meanders through soft glacial deposits, but the railway cuttings reveal hard, black mudstones, which have been more resistant to erosion. The Wescoe Tunnel cuts through a massive outcrop of mudstone.

WALK I:
The Railway Route

Length: 5.5 miles

Start: Keswick railway station

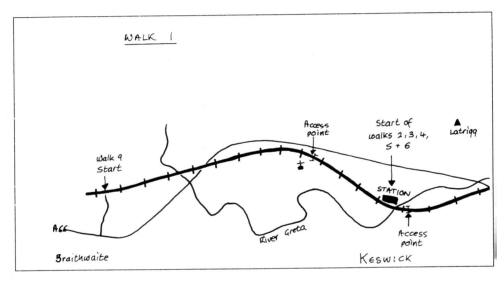

This section traces the route of the CKPR from Keswick eastwards to Threlkeld (the best maintained section, and suitable
for the disabled and elderly, not requiring special footwear) and
westwards towards Braithwaite. Each walk in the book will
begin on a section of this route, before heading off in a circuit
back to the starting point. It is possible also to walk the whole
of this section, or just pick a section and walk it both ways.
Possible access points onto the railway and the points where
the walks branch off will be noted.

Keswick Station

Many of the railway walks start from Keswick Station, where there is ample car parking. The station buildings are still intact, and have been restored in their original style with a glass canopy and seats on the platform. These buildings for a time operated as a restaurant, but at the time of writing are again

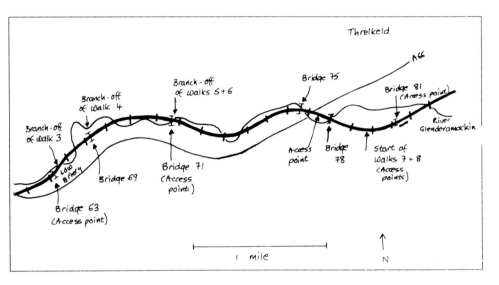

vacant. Nearby is the Keswick Hotel, built in the late 1860s, shortly after the railway line opened. The site of the old goods yard is now occupied by the Leisure Spa.

The lands acquired for Keswick Station were purchased from General le Fleming, and the contract to build it was placed in 1863. As can be seen today, it had a west-east alignment, with a single line and platform running in each direction, and access to the goods yard at the western end. The upstairs of the station housed the Boardroom of the CKPR and Manager's Office, with a ticket office and waiting rooms downstairs. From 1869 until the 1950s, the platform had a bookstall run at various times by

W.H. Smith's, Chaplin's (both still in Keswick) and Wyman and Sons. At the eastern end of the platform, a pair of double doors marks the point of a subway through to the Keswick Hotel. If this is open, the stained glass portraits of artists are worth noting. Electricity was added in 1899, the only CKPR station (except Penrith) to receive it, and telephones were installed in 1910.

Ironstone and coke passed through the goods station. There once was a timber weigh-bridge cabin, and a stone goods shed, which is now the leisure pool. Two signal boxes existed, and workshops and stores for plumbers, joiners and blacksmiths.

Walk 2 is a circular walk from the Station, and goes into more detail regarding the Station and Keswick Hotel.

Keswick Station to Low Briery Bobbin Mill

Begin walking from Keswick Station, down the platform in an easterly direction. Milepost 13 was located here (13 miles from Cockermouth Junction). This section, to Threlkeld, includes some breath-taking scenery through the Greta Gorge. "Trains travelled too quickly for the appreciation of two short tunnels and fully a dozen bridges – including eight spectacular bow-string girder underline bridges by which the single track rail-way crossed and recrossed the rocky river valley. A platelayer's eye view, or that of the walker today, is however rewarding" (Bowtell, 1989).

From the eastern end of the platform, looking north, it is easy to imagine trains still pulling in to Keswick Station. Although the Down line and platform (western platform) are still intact, little remains of the Up platform (eastern side) which had limited facilities, and a water tower. This now forms part of the car park. Continue past the Keswick Hotel on the right, and the timeshare apartments on the left. Cross the first of many bow-string girder bridges, over the River Greta (a Norse word meaning 'Rocky Stream') and the A591. This bridge – number 59 or Stank Dub – is an example of a pair of inverted bow-strings, and a detour on the left towards the timeshare apartments shows clearly the massive steel centre-plate girder, added in 1933 for strengthening, thus allowing larger locomotives to run on the line. Looking westwards from the bridge, the River Greta flows quietly into Keswick, and looking eastwards, or upstream, the eye is drawn into the Greta Gorge, by the slopes of Latrigg, past the old packhorse Calvert's Bridge.

Proceed over a smaller bridge leading down to Brigham (access point). On the right stands the new infants school, opened in September 1993 for all the younger children in Keswick, next to the junior school opened in 1973/74, again replacing several smaller schools. On the left are the houses of Latrigg Close, and behind them the slopes of Latrigg, nestling underneath Skiddaw. The line then passes underneath a rather suburban-looking bridge (re-built in 1992) carrying the A591 (access point) before climbing up to a plateau. This has superb views to the west and east. This plateau is the top of the long railway tunnel, filled in when the A66 was built. The line went through the tunnel, and down to the banks of the river to 'Big Tunnel', also infilled. Follow the path, crossing underneath the massive A66 fly-over bridge (built in 1976, towering over the houses at The Forge below), and up the hill to the A66, before plummeting into the Greta Gorge and its gurgling river. This leads the walker into an insulated, almost secret, valley with tantalising views emerging from tunnels of trees and rock. Arriving at the bottom of the path from the A66, the old route of the railway towards Big Tunnel can be seen, but this is now blocked off. Ahead, the path runs on a rocky shelf alongside the river, the eye being drawn up the gorge towards Saddleback or Blencathra.

Pass under a stone arched bridge (No 63, carrying a road to Low Briery), and immediately on the left is the old Briery Platform (access point). At this point, a loop in the river provided the site for a bobbin mill and cottages, and a display board narrates the story of this site. At its peak, the bobbin mill produced over 40 million bobbins a year, or a production line 800 miles long, before closing in 1961. In the 1820s, the mill manufactured waistcoats and woollens, bobbin-making coming in the 1830s. Trains called daily for the workmen, to deliver timber or collect bobbins, until November 1958. The mill buildings and workers' cottages have now been adapted to provide holiday accommodation, and directly behind the platform, lies a caravan site.

Low Briery to Threlkeld

Continue from Low Briery, in a short while crossing an inverted bow-string bridge (curved bow below) over the gushing River Greta. At the end of the bridge, on the left, a path leads off past Low Briery (Walk 3). The railway line then enters an enclosed section, but in Spring this harbours beautiful flowers. Cross another inverted bow-string bridge with the river meandering back to the left of the path, and the scene opens, revealing a wide flood plain and meadow on the left. (A fisherman's path runs down along this plain and the banks of the river on the left until the next bridge, allowing a shorter circuit to be followed if wanted). There is then a long stretch of line through enclosed woodland, with evidence of past coppicing for the bobbin mill. Also look out for a white half-mile post, denoting $14\frac{1}{2}$ miles from Cockermouth Junction.

The next bridge, number 69 at White Moss, is different to

those previously encountered, as it is an upright bow-string girder, with the curved boom being above the line.

old railway bridge

It has been suggested that the railway engineer preferred the inverted arrangement, but this was not possible here because of lack of clearance above the river bed at high water. At the end of this bridge, on the left, is a footpath marked 'Brundholme Woods' (Walk 4). The route continues, leaving another woodland area, and entering into a stretch of open fields, with extensive views towards the mountains. It is easy to see how this route remains undiscovered by so many, running unobtrusively, as it does along the bottom of this secret gorge. Shortly, you will encounter an old station hut – an ideal place to stop and enjoy your refreshments, while also reading display boards inside about the River Greta, the bird life, and the National Park.

Old Station Hut

Immediately after the hut is bridge 71 – Brundholme Bridge – with a 100 ft span, and additional side struts. At the beginning of the bridge, a footpath leads off on the left to Latrigg (Walk 5), and at the end of the bridge, on the right, another path is marked to Castlerigg Stone Circle (Walks 6 & 7). Note the delightful packhorse bridge on the left (access point), and the views towards Skiddaw and Saddleback (and the old Sanatorium, now an outdoor field centre).

Continue along the route, through another enclosed stretch, and look out for a white half-mile post on the left, representing 15¼ miles from Cockermouth Junction (or 2½ miles from Keswick Station). The route crosses bridge 72, over Naddle Beck, followed by bridge 73 – Rowsome, another inverted bow-string, also showing massive strengthening from 1926, with a deep central girder and additional stays. The river gurgles and gushes away on the right, and this makes another excellent place to enjoy a picnic or snack.

The next feature of interest is a tunnel, the only one remaining on this stretch of the CKPR. Through the damp tunnel can be glimpsed another upright bridge, Number 74, this time with strengthening girders across the top of the bridge, and outrigger stays. Continue on, flanked by Wescoe Wood on the left, and Burns Wood on the right. Pass milepost 15½, and you will come across another station hut. This contains information on the establishment and closure of the railway, and the tea and religious ministrations given to the navvies to keep them calm!

Finally, bridge 75 – Crozier Holme is reached, strengthened in 1931. If you wish to walk to Threlkeld (access point, a small village with a church, post office and pubs), continue along the bridge. This was the route of the old railway, but part of the section has been infilled to make way for the A66. To continue along the line towards Threlkeld Station and Penrith, take the footpath on the right, just before the bridge. This path leads down to the banks of the river, where there is a wonderful contrast between the A66 concrete bridge and behind it Threlkeld Bridge, an old stone bridge which carried the main road to Keswick before the A66. At this point, the River Glenderamackin and St John's Beck merge. The path comes out onto the road through two gates just before the bridge. Turn left and walk along the road a few yards. Before the bend, there is a gate and footpath marker on the right – this allows access to the CKP line again.

Continue along the line, crossing bridge 78 – Screw Ghyll (a screw pile bridge where cast iron piles were screwed into the ground) over the River Glenderamackin (rebuilt in 1936). To the west, Naddle Fell can be seen, and in the east Skiddaw, Saddleback and Threlkeld Village. Shortly on the left, is milepost 16¼. The line then comes to a halt, as the bridge over the Thirlmere road has been removed. Note the National Park board showing the railway route to Keswick. To re-join the line, pass through the gates and take the path on the left down to the road. Cross the road, and there is a path on the right back up to the line (access point, and walks 7 & 8).

The path narrows now but leads on past the National Park works and storage depot on the site of the old Threlkeld Station. This was demolished between 1985 – 86, although part of the platform is still evident. The Station Master's House, built in 1865 still stands, a white house on the left at the end of the depot; and next to it, a pair of railwaymen's cottages. Threlkeld Station was originally on the single line, but in 1892, it was converted to an insular platform, the only one on the CKPR route to take the form of two platforms facing an island. An unusual feature was the signal-box, part of the platform buildings at the western end. The station also had a goods yard (in the 1890s this received masonry, pipes and valves to be used by Manchester Corporation in building the dam and aqueduct at Thirlmere), sidings for Threlkeld Quarry traffic, and a linking route to the Quarries in St John's in-the-Vale.

Proceed along the line, under bridge 81 – the spidery 'fly' bridge (access point) – the fragile construction of which led to plans for its replacement in 1935, but the work was never done. On the right are more railway houses – Railway Terrace, now called Glenderamackin Terrace, completed in the 1890s, and behind this 'Top Row', now Blencathra View, dating from the early 1880s. The Quarry also had a small school, Chapel, cricket and football grounds (see Walk 8 for more information). Further on to one's right are some new workshops – the Blencathra Business Centre, on the site of the old sidings. These were opened in December 1990 by Prince Charles, and house a range of businesses, such as upholstery, and a food distributor and wholesalers. There are superb views from here, over towards Threlkeld, and the mountains beyond.

It used to be possible to walk the line another two miles, to Guardhouse. Now however, access is only possible up to the golf course. Continue until the next bridge – a stone and metal arched construction, engraved 'Pratchitt Brothers, Carlisle,

1893'. This is as far as one can walk now, the rest of the line being fenced off (Walk 8). From here, the railway used to extend to Troutbeck (880ft) – 400 ft of climbing in 4¾ miles, over Mosedale viaduct, and onto Penruddock, Blencow and then Penrith.

Keswick Station towards Braithwaite

Unfortunately, access along the line westwards to Braithwaite is only possible for half the original distance. From Keswick Station walk westwards, past the leisure pool on the site of the old goods yard. On the far right behind the trees, is the Station House, built in 1865, now providing bed and breakfast accommodation. Proceed on through a small housing estate (North and Impact Housing, opened in 1990), and follow a path on the left leading down into Fitz Park for a short while, before re-joining the line after the housing estate. Fitz Park allows the appreciation of superb views over towards the Newlands Valley. This section of the line is rather wild, and obviously not used or developed as much as the route eastwards. On the right are the houses of Briar Rigg, and behind them, the slopes of Latrigg.

After a short distance the path descends, as the bridge over the lane to Briar Rigg has been removed. Continue on a path next to this lane, towards the A591. Cross the main road by the Pheasant Inn, and walk towards the roundabout. The railway used to cross the A591 opposite the Pheasant, by an underline bridge. Near the roundabout on the left, just beyond Vicarage Hill, the railway route can again be followed, it is well-signed. This section is a woodland section, again more overgrown, and wetter underfoot than the eastern stretch. Pass the quarter-mile post on the right, denoting 12¼ miles from Cockermouth Junction. Cross a small bridge, with a footpath leading to Thrushwood on the right. From here, there are again good views towards Skiddaw.

Continue to bridge 52, by Crosthwaite Churchyard (see walk 2; access point). The route then crosses through the churchyard, and in a short while comes out onto the A66 road. This is the furthest the line can be walked in this direction. Its previous route can be seen ahead, but most of the bridges have been removed, making further walking impossible. From here, the line used to go to Braithwaite Station (see walk 9), and goods yard (closed in 1966), and on to Bassenthwaite Lake and Embleton, before reaching Cockermouth. Cockermouth Station provided a link to Workington. The Cockermouth to Keswick section of the line closed in 1966.

Bibliography

Bowtell, Harold D.: **Rails through Lakeland**. An illustrated history of the Workington-Cockermouth-Keswick-Penrith Railway, 1887 – 1972. Silver Link Publishing Ltd: Kettering. 1989

WALK 2:
The Keswick Circle

Length: 2.5 miles

Start: Keswick railway station

This walk follows the railway route from Keswick Station to Crosthwaite Church, and then takes a footpath through the fields behind High Hill; it returns to the station, noting various points of railway and town history along the way.

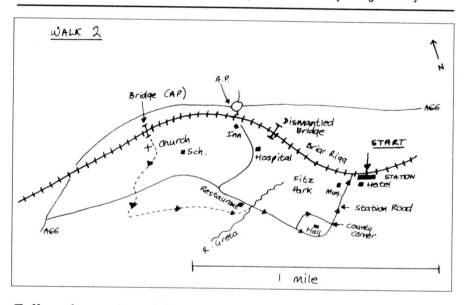

Follow the section of the railway route described in Walk 1 from Keswick Station westwards towards Braithwaite, as far as bridge 52 by Crosthwaite Church. At the bridge, there is a path down to the road on the right. Turn left underneath the bridg , towards the Church. Crosthwaite Church, or St Kentigern's was said to have been founded by Kentigern/Mungo in 553 AD, when he placed his cross in a clearing or thwaite. The oldest part of the Church dates from 1191 AD. The brass rubbings of the Radcliffe family (the late Earl of Derwentwater, and original owners of the Moot Hall) can be found here, and the grave of the poet Robert Southey. On the left are the playing fields and buildings of Lairthwaite School, now the lower site of Keswick Secondary School. Next to the Church, is the old primary school, currently being used by Keswick School as a domestic science and sewing block.

Turn right, past the Church and school buildings and onto a footpath towards Portinscale, emerging next to the A66. Cross over the A66 and turn right towards Portinscale, and in a short distance, take the footpath on the left through the gate, just before the suspension bridge. Follow this path, through the open fields, with good views on the left of Skiddaw, Latrigg and Keswick and, on the right, over to Newlands and Catbells. The path leads onto a track by the side of the River Greta. Turn left, past the Italian Restaurant and onto the main road. Turn right, over Greta Bridge. Opposite stands the Cumberland Pencil Mill and museum, the World's first pencil factory, established in 1566.

Continue along the road, past Keswick School on the left, and the old bus station on the right (now the Lakes Food Store) and on into town. Follow the road round to the left at the Post Office and up the hill towards County Corner with its war memorial, erected in 1923 by the Wivells of the Keswick Hotel. At County Corner, turn left down Station Road (relevant to Walk 6 also), constructed by the Railway Company, sweeping past the goods yard (now the Leisure Spa) and up to the spacious station forecourt and Keswick Hotel. A secondary road was also built behind the hotel, leading to the coach houses and stables, and onto the Station Master's house. On the back of the war memorial is a plaque of the CKPR dedicated to its employees who died in the First World War. This used to be located on the front wall of the station, but was relocated in 1972.

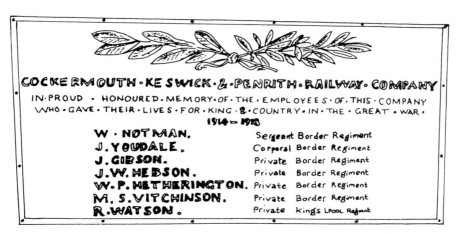

COCKERMOUTH·KESWICK·&·PENRITH·RAILWAY·COMPANY·
IN·PROUD · HONOURED·MEMORY·OF·THE·EMPLOYEES·OF·THIS·COMPANY
WHO·GAVE·THEIR·LIVES·FOR·KING·&·COUNTRY·IN·THE·GREAT·WAR·
1914 – 1918

W · NOTMAN.	Sergeant	Border	Regiment
J. YOUDALE.	Corporal	Border	Regiment
J. GIBSON.	Private	Border	Regiment
J.W. HEBSON.	Private	Border	Regiment
W. P. HETHERINGTON.	Private	Border	Regiment
M. S. VITCHINSON.	Private	Border	Regiment
R. WATSON.	Private	Kings	Lpool Regiment

Memorial plaque

Continue down Station Road, and on the right, just before the bridge, you will pass a drinking fountain, placed by Edward Grayson in 1865. Further on is Higher Fitz Park on the right, with gates dating from 1882, and Lower Fitz Park on the left, dating from the early 1880s, and developed on land bought from the Keswick Hotel. The Museum on the left dates from 1887, and houses the manuscripts of local poets, a good mineral collection, and the 'musical stones'. Just past the museum, on the left near the pavement is a memorial stone to the CK and PR, a boundary stone.

CK&PR
CO*

Boundary stone

Proceed on towards the Keswick Hotel. On the left is the Leisure Spa on the site of the old goods yard, weighbridge, and workshops. The road ends in a forecourt, with the station buildings on the left, and the Keswick Hotel up ahead. The station was the headquarters of the CKPR

Board of Directors, and then the London-Midland service until 1939. In the upstairs west wing, the Boardroom was located, next to the Secretary's office. The Traffic Manager was housed under the next gable, and the Accountant resided in the east wing. The lower floor contained the ticket office, waiting room and other premises. There was a Refreshment Room, but it survived only until 1873, and then became a first-class waiting room for gentlemen! The front portico was changed to a plain glazed room and the present green and cream colours were adopted around 1960. Famous visitors to the station included Kaiser Wilhelm in August 1885 for tea and the Queen in October 1956 with the Royal Train.

In 1873, a subway was built between the platforms and the Keswick Hotel, and a stained glass screen depicting various artists can still be seen from the platform to the hotel conservatory.

The Hotel was built on 3.5 acres of land from General le Fleming, at a cost of £12,000, and opened in 1865, although it was not completed until later. The 'Keswick Hotel Company' was established from 1866, and it purchased the estate from the CKPR. It was run by the Wivells, who later owned the Armathwaite Hall Hotel, and during the war housed Roedean School girls. In 1945 the Wivells sold the hotel, and since then there have been various owners. The Keswick hotels gained most of their business from the railway, and most commissioned horse drawn omnibuses to meet the trains. For example, in 1921, hotels with stands included the Royal Oak and Queens, Lodging Houses, King's Arms, George Hotel, Blencathra and Park, Derwentwater Hotel, Lodore, Lake Hotel, Skiddaw and County.

From the Keswick Hotel, continue the walk back to the station – take a path past the right-hand side of the Hotel, through the gardens. This is well-signed. It leads onto the road, past the

Keswick Hotel Garage. Pass under the railway bridge, and then take the path on the right leading onto the railway line. Walk back westwards towards the station platform.

WALK 3:
Low Briery

Length: 2.5 miles

Start: Keswick railway station

This is one of the shorter walks, tracing the railway line from Keswick Station to Low Briery, crossing the river, and returning via the woods and Forge Brow.

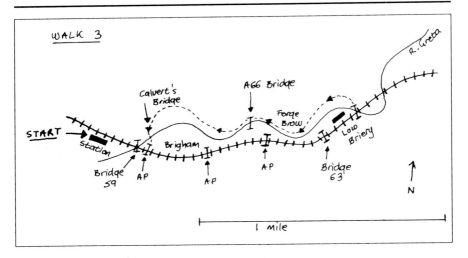

Start from Keswick Station, and follow the railway eastwards as outlined in Walk 1, until the bridge just after the Low Briery Mill platform. At the end of the bridge, on the left, a path leads down towards the river bank. Follow this through the woodland towards Keswick. This path is well-marked (and links in with walks 4 and 5), but can be rather wet underfoot. There is a good view across the river towards the Low Briery mill site, where the mill buildings and workmen's cottages have been renovated to form holiday accommodation.

Continue along the path, and you will pass under the A66 bridge again (links in with walk 4). Opposite, the original route of the railway down towards the river and through Big Tunnel is more obvious. On the right are the houses and mill houses of the Forge. Proceed on, and the path will wind its way down to a packhorse bridge over the river at the Forge. There are now two choices – to walk through the gate at the Forge and rejoin the railway line near Latrigg Close – or to continue through the woods towards Greta Bank and the Station.

Forge Bridge

a. Via the Forge and Latrigg Close

Continue towards the gate next to the packhorse bridge. Turn left over the bridge, passing the houses and old mill units of the Forge (once used as a corn mill, a bobbin mill, and for smelting and processing copper ore). Shortly after this, next to a passing place, a well-marked path on the left rejoins the railway line. Alternatively, continue until the road joins the A591; turn left up the hill, and just before the bridge, take the steps down to the railway line on the left. Turn right, and walk back westwards towards the Station.

b. Forge Brow and Greta Bank

Before the packhorse bridge, follow a path (well marked) leading up some wooden steps on the right. This leads through Forge Brow woods, coming out at the Calvert Trust's riding centre at Windebrowe. Turn left on to the road, and follow it past the Brundholme Country Guest House on the left (ignore the footpath sign here). Shortly after this, take the signed footpath on the left. This leads down through the woods, under a bridge, and comes out on an old packhorse bridge – Calvert's Bridge at Brigham. Cross the main road, and take the path behind the right-hand side of the petrol station, leading back on to the railway. Turn right, and return to the Station.

WALK 4:
Brundholme Woods

Length: 3.5 – 4 miles

Start: Keswick railway station

This is a longer version of Walk 3: a delightful mix of the linear railway route from Keswick Station and a winding path through Brundholme Woods.

Start from Keswick Station, and follow the railway line as far as bridge 69 at White Moss, as described in Walk 1. At the end of this bridge, on the left, is a path signed 'Keswick via Brundholme Woods'. This leads down to a meadowy field, and up an incline to the wood. It is a well-marked path (yellow posts), linking into one to Latrigg, but can be rather wet and muddy. At the top of the incline, turn left over the stile, towards Keswick. The path often diverges, but all the routes lead in the same direction. This route has wonderful views, back down towards the railway line and River Greta.

Follow the path through the woods and you will come out under the A66 fly-over bridge again. Turn to Walk 3 (para 2) where the rest of this walk is described in detail.

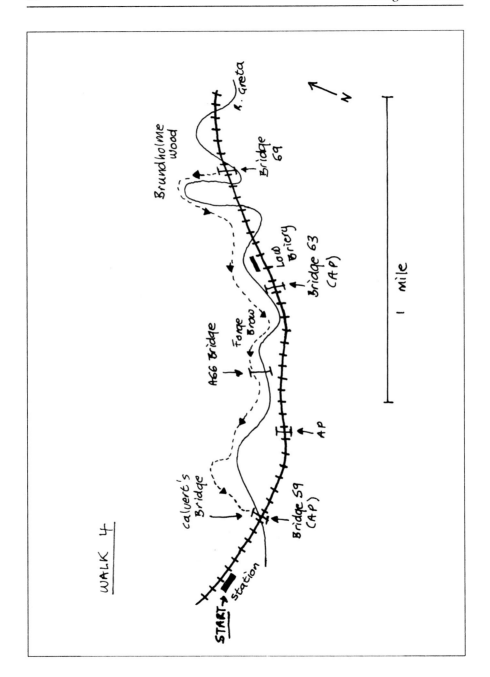

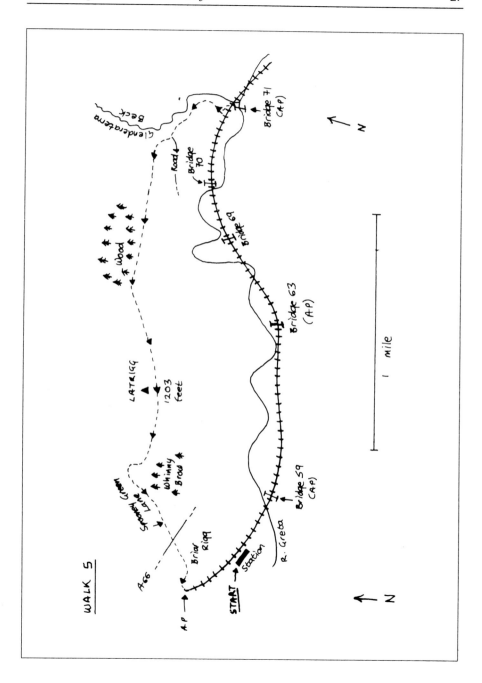

WALK 5:
Latrigg

Length: 5.5 miles

Start: Keswick railway station

This is the most strenuous walk in the book, following the railway line from Keswick towards Threlkeld, and then climbing to the summit of Latrigg, and down towards Briar Rigg and the Station. It is however well worthwhile for its wonderful views and variety of terrain.

Start from Keswick Station, and follow the railway route towards Threlkeld as far as Brundholme Bridge (71), as described in Walk 1. At the start of this bridge on the left, follow the sign marked 'Keswick via Latrigg, Blencathra'.

The path leads alongside the Glenderaterra Beck and the packhorse bridge. At the bridge, turn left onto the lane, and follow this up the hill, past the white house on the left. Proceed past the sign to Blencathra, and at the top of the hill, veer left towards a sign on the right to 'Skiddaw and Underscar'. Follow this path, round the back of the lower slopes of Latrigg up to a gate with a wood on your left. There are wonderful views in all directions, and the path of the railway line in the Greta Gorge below can be clearly seen. Through the gate, veer left slightly, and the path begins to follow the ridge of Latrigg. Pass through a stile near the pine trees which are a distinctive feature of Latrigg, and the summit is straight ahead.

On the summit (1203 feet), admire the views in all directions, a panorama of mountains and lakes, valleys and plains. Continue from the summit westwards, down the edge of the ridge. Ignore the path on the right near the seat, and head straight down the ridge, which is quite steep in places. Eventually, you will reach a gate, and after passing through this will come out near Whinny Brow woods. Turn right on to a forestry track, and follow this round in an 'S' bend and down the hill. From here there are beautiful views up to Bassenthwaite Lake and plains. Go through a gate on to Spooney Green Lane; cross the bridge over the A66, and you will come out on the Briar Rigg road.

Turn right on to the road and, just after the houses, near the site of the old railway bridge, take a path on the left leading up to the railway line. Follow this, and where new houses block your way, head through a kissing gate on the right into Fitz Park. After a short distance, there is another kissing gate on the left, which leads through the housing estate and back to the Leisure Spa and the Station.

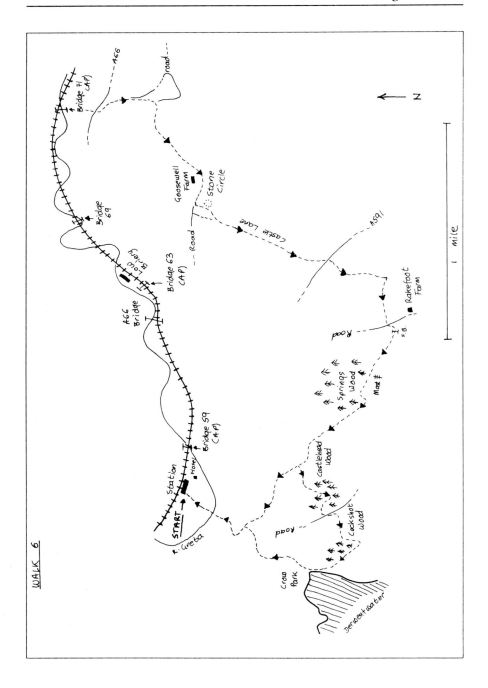

WALK 6:
Keswick
and the
Castlerigg Stone Circle

Length: 5.5 miles

Start: Keswick railway station

This is a longer walk, from Keswick Station, along the railway line, and then up to Castlerigg Stone Circle, before returning to Keswick across the fields via Rakefoot and Springs Wood.

Begin from Keswick Station, and follow the railway route eastwards towards Threlkeld as described in Walk 1, until Brundholme Bridge (71). Cross the bridge, and immediately on the right, take the path signed 'A66 road, Castlerigg Stone Circle'.

Follow this path along the banks of the Greta, and up the hill in a straight line, coming out at the A66. Take time to look back at the marvellous views of the Greta Gorge, Saddleback, Skiddaw and Latrigg.

Towards Saddleback

Cross the A66, and turn right. After a few yards, follow the wooden footpath sign on the left, leading up the road banking, and coming out on the old Keswick to Penrith road. Turn left and follow the road, until a right-hand turn signed to Castlerigg Stone Circle. Take this road, leading up the hill, past Goosewell Farm on the right, and towards the 50 stones at the stone circle on the brow of the hill. The stone circle is 700 feet above sea-level, and has been owned by the National Trust since 1913.

It is thought to have been built in 1400 BC, for bartering, exchanges, celebrations of tribal festivals and to tell the seasons. There are wonderful panoramic views to be seen from here.

Walk through the stones, towards the top right-hand corner of the field (looking south), and over a stone stile in the wall onto Castle Lane. Turn left, and walk along the lane for half a mile until it joins the A591 Keswick to Windermere road. Cross the road, and head through the gate opposite, signed 'Rake-foot'. Continue straight ahead, keeping close to the wall bordering the fields. This is a well-signed path, turning right towards Keswick after three fields, again next to the wall boundary. When the path joins the lane, turn left; after a few yards, take the path signed 'Keswick and Great Wood', leading down to a wooden bridge over Brockle Beck. Cross the footbridge and turn right, descending through the woods, with the beck below on your right. After the second kissing gate, continue straight on down the hill (the path on the left leads to Great Wood and Borrowdale), with wonderful views over Derwentwater towards Borrowdale and Newlands. Pass the mast on your left, and follow the path down, through a kissing gate into the farm yard of Springs Farm.

Castlerigg Stone Circle

Pass between the two barns, and turn right over the pack-horse bridge onto Springs Road. Proceed along this road, with the houses on your right, and Castle Head and its woodland on your left. There is now a choice of route – back to the Station via town or via the lake shore and boat landings.

a. Via Keswick

At the road junction, turn left, towards Keswick, passing St John's Church, and the primary school (closed in summer 1993, the children now attending the new infants school you passed earlier near Latrigg Close). Opposite the school is the old library, for a time used as part of the school. Continue into Keswick. At the next major junction (next to Dixons newsagents), turn right into Station Road, and continue across the road at County Corner to return to the Station. You may observe several railway monuments and the Keswick Hotel, noted towards the end of Walk 2.

b. Via Derwentwater and the landing stages

Before Springs Road joins the road into Keswick, take a path on the left towards Castle Head. Follow this straight path, and then it is worth just climbing up to the summit of Castle Head for wonderful views over Derwentwater. The path leads down the other side of the hill to the main Borrowdale road. Cross this road, and take the path opposite, leading to Cockshot Wood. Turn left and follow the outer edge of the wood, leading down to the lake shore and the boat landings on the right. Follow the road past the old Century Theatre on your right, and Hope Park on the left, and through the subway into Lake Road. Turn left at the top of Lake Road, near Fishers, leading to market square. Turn left here, and left again, into Station Road. At the County

Corner cross roads, continue straight across to the Station. You may observe several railway monuments, and the Keswick Hotel, described at the end of Walk 2.

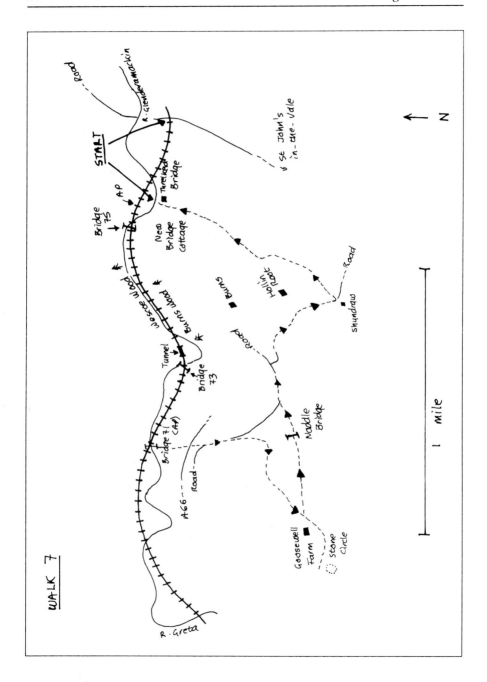

WALK 7:
Threlkeld
to
Castlerigg Stone Circle

Length: 5 miles

Start: Threlkeld station

Walks 7 and 8 start from the Threlkeld end of the railway line. This walk proceeds from Threlkeld towards Keswick along the railway line, and up to Castlerigg Stone Circle, before returning through the fields to Threlkeld.

The walk begins from the site of the old bridge over the St John's-in-the-Vale road near Threlkeld Station; OR from Threlkeld Bridge near New Bridge Cottage if you wish to shorten it slightly. Walk along the railway line westwards towards Keswick, as described towards the end of Walk 1 but in reverse, as far as Brundholme Bridge (No 71).

Just before this bridge, there is a footpath sign on the left marked 'Castlerigg Stone Circle'. Follow this path, over the stile and along the river bank, then up the hill until it joins the A66. There are wonderful views here towards Saddleback, Latrigg and Skiddaw.

Towards Latrigg

Cross the A66, and walk westwards, towards Keswick. Shortly on the left, there is a footpath sign, pointing up the banking. Follow this route, coming out on the old Keswick to Penrith main road. Turn left, and continue along the road until the next junction, where a road leads off on the right, signed Castlerigg Stone Circle. Follow this road up the hill, past Goosewell Farm, and on the left at the top of the hill you will find the Stone Circle. This was built in 1400 BC, and was originally used as a place to barter, celebrate tribal festivals, and establish the seasons. It is 700 feet above sea-level, has 50 stones in total, and has been owned by the National Trust since 1913. It is worth taking time to admire the views in all directions: north to Bassenthwaite, Skiddaw, Latrigg and Saddleback; east to Penrith and Mell Fell; south to the Naddle Valley and Helvellyn range; and west towards Borrowdale and round to Newlands.

Retrace your steps down towards Goosewell Farm. Just opposite the farm, take the footpath on the right. This leads down through the fields, coming out next to Naddle Bridge. Turn right onto the road, and follow the road round onto the old main road. Take the next turn right, signed Shundraw and St John's in-the-Vale Church.

Continue along this road, with beautiful views down St John's in-the-Vale towards Castle Crag and the Helvellyn range. At the bottom of the hill, opposite Shundraw Farm, take the footpath on the left through the gate. Cross the field diagonally, towards Threlkeld, to a wigwam stile. Continue in the same direction, towards the next gate (this section can be muddy). Head eastwards, following a straight line through the middle of three fields, and then bear left and slightly upwards, coming out next to New Bridge Cottage and Threlkeld Bridge on the old main road. Turn right onto the road, and take the path shortly on the right, leading back onto the railway line, and the start of the walk.

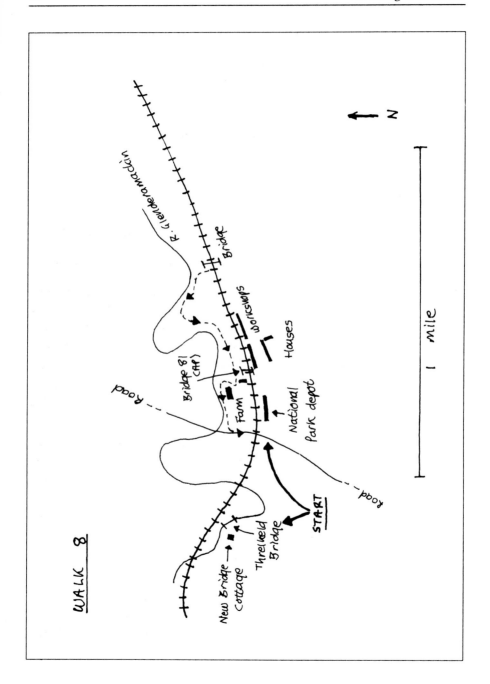

WALK 8:
Threlkeld
and
the River Glenderamackin

Length: 1.5 miles

Start: Threlkeld Station

This is one of the shorter walks and is very pleasant for a summer evening. It follows a circle from Threlkeld Station, along the railway, and back by the banks of the River Glenderamackin.

Join the railway at the site of the old bridge over the road to St John's-in-the-Vale, next to Threlkeld Station; OR at Threlkeld Bridge near New Bridge Cottage if you wish to extend the walk slightly. Walk along the route towards the station, now a National Park depot. Part of the old platform is still visible, but little else of the station or its extensive goods yard and sidings remain. Follow this part of the route as described towards the end of Walk 1.

A small detour can be made up and across the spidery fly bridge (bridge 81) or via steps and a path just beyond this, up to the railway cottages on the right-hand side of the line. The bottom row of houses, once 'Railway Terrace', now called 'Glenderamackin Terrace' was completed in the late 1890s, and has wonderful views towards Threlkeld and Saddleback.

This row housed the Company offices, and contained six of the most dignified houses. Walk up the hill southwards past the end of Glenderamackin Terrace, and you will pass the old Wesleyan Chapel, opened in 1903, and converted into a house in 1981. Turn left down 'Blencathra View', once called 'Top

Row', and comprising 12 tin houses and 6 narrow stone houses, dating from the early 1880s. At the start of this row is the old school, now a dwelling. 100 children attended the Quarry School, but by 1951, only 11 attended, and it closed. The quarry village also had a reading room, lodging house, horse-keepers house, stables, cricket and football grounds.

Glenderamackin Terrace

Continue along to the end of this row, from where the old quarry can clearly be seen. These quarries supplied the biggest part of the CKPR's freight in the 1920s. A track also ran into St John's-in-the-Vale to the quarries there. Complete closure took place in 1981.

Turn left, down the hill to the last of the houses, and then right, along the road. Pass through the gate ahead, towards the new workshops, opened in 1990 by Prince Charles. These are on the site of the old goods yard and sidings. At the end of the workshops, go through the gate ahead, and over a small stile on the left next to an old shed, to rejoin the railway line.

Continue along the line eastwards as far as you can, before the route is fenced off at the bridge inscribed 'Pratchitt Brothers, Carlisle 1893'. Turn left, through the kissing gate, and left onto a small road leading downhill towards Threlkeld. Just before the bridge over the River Glenderamackin, take the footpath signed on the left through the gate. Follow the path, keeping next to the fence, with the river on your right. The path leads round the field, and comes out near the river bank. Take the slate stile to the right of the gate in the wall ahead, cross over the footbridge, and turn right onto the rough track. Continue along the track, and pass through the gate or stile, with Setmabanning farm buildings on your right. Just after the gate, turn right into the farm yard (the spidery fly bridge is on your left), and right again between two barns. Pass through the farm yard gates (which are sometimes closed) and turn left, past a barn; you will come out onto a track behind the farm, with the river flowing below you on the right. Continue along the track westwards, past the farm and caravan park, down to the banks of the river. The path will lead you to an old picket gate joining the St John's in-the-Vale road. Turn left, and you will return to the dismantled bridge near the station (or re-join the railway on the right if you wish to return to Threlkeld Bridge). On the left, you can clearly see the black and white railway houses – on the left 1 and 2 Railway Cottages and, nearest to the railway line, the Station House, dating from 1865. All these houses are occupied today.

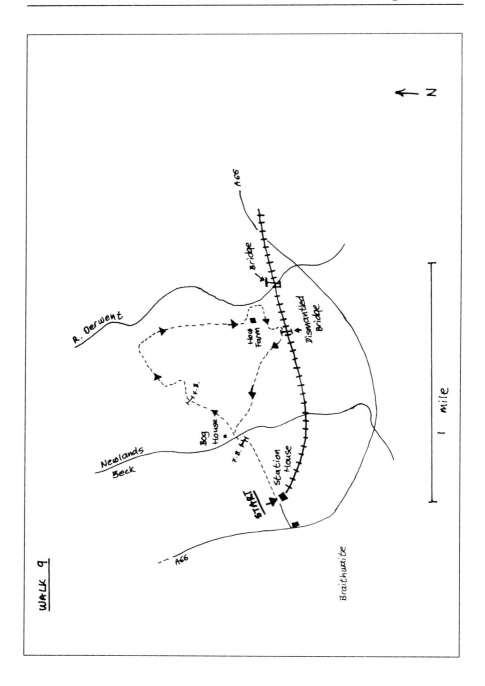

WALK 9:
A Circuit from
Braithwaite Station

Length: 2.5 miles

Start: Braithwaite Station

This is really the only feasible circular walk I could find from the Braithwaite end of the railway. The A66 uses most of the old line west of Braithwaite, and the eastern section up to Crosthwaite is not accessible as many of the bridges have been dismantled. This walk however begins from Braithwaite Station, and crosses the fields towards Millbeck, runs south onto the Allerdale Ramble, and back towards Braithwaite. It is an easy lowland walk, affording beautiful views in all directions.

Braithwaite Station

Begin from Braithwaite Station. This is reached by taking a narrow lane off the A66, on the right (running towards Cockermouth), just after the Village Institute. At the end of the lane are some farm buildings and the old Station House. This is a beautiful house, and the owners have made a feature of the old platform, incorporating it as part of their house and garden.

The Station House was extended in 1889, and even then was known for its garden and flower beds. The Station Master won many prizes for the 'best kept section of railway'. On the eastern side of the house, there used to be a goods yard behind the platform, and sidings and a warehouse for Thornthwaite Mines Ltd who operated through the station.

From behind the Station House, cross over the stile in the fence opposite, and proceed straight ahead in the direction of Skiddaw.

Towards Skiddaw

The path follows an almost straight line across the field, over two ditches, and then branches left to the footbridge over Newlands Beck (it is well signposted). Follow the signs for Dancing Gate, and continue past the Bog House and through a reedy meadow, before turning left to the next footbridge. From the bridge head straight across the fields, crossing two more footbridges. Follow the path on the right marked Portinscale (part of the Allerdale Ramble), up to How Farm. Beautiful views can be observed in all directions. Just before the farm gates, take a path through a stile on the left, leading down to the River Derwent (bypassing the farm yard). Bear right, and cross over the stile, observing one of the old railway bridges up ahead. Turn right, and head towards a gate at the top of the field, next to the houses, leading onto a small lane.

Cross the road, and taking the footpath opposite, walk down through the fields, bearing slightly left. Enjoy the beautiful views towards Grizedale and Causey Pikes. The path goes through a gate (it can be very muddy here), and branches left over a small beck. You can again observe the railway line and site of an old bridge on the left. Veer right, along the side of the stream (not along the track straight ahead). After a while, look out for a sign pointing to a gap in the trees on the left (not obvious). Go through the gap, and bear right to a stile and footbridge. After crossing the bridge, head over the field to join a track in the far corner. Turn right along the track, returning to the bridge over Newlands Beck, and retrace your steps back to Braithwaite Station and your starting point.

We publish guides to individual towns, plus books on walking and cycling in the great outdoors throughout England and Wales. This is a recent selection:

The Lake District

FULL DAYS ON THE FELLS – Adrian Dixon (£7.95)
100 LAKE DISTRICT HILL WALKS – Gordon Brown *(£7.95)*
LAKELAND ROCKY RAMBLES: Geology beneath your feet – Brian Lynas *(£9.95)*
PUB WALKS IN THE LAKE DISTRICT – Neil Coates *(£6.95)*
LAKELAND WALKING, ON THE LEVEL – Norman Buckley *(£6.95)*
MOSTLY DOWNHILL: LEISURELY WALKS, LAKE DISTRICT – Alan Pears *(£6.95)*
THE THIRLMERE WAY – Tim Cappelli *(£6.95)*
THE FURNESS TRAIL – Tim Cappelli *(£6.95)*
CYCLING IN THE LAKE DISTRICT – John Wood *(£7.95)*

Other destinations . . .

LOG BOOK OF THE MOUNTAINS OF ENGLAND – Mark Woosey (£9.95)
LOG BOOK OF THE MOUNTAINS OF WALES – Mark Woosey (£7.95)
FIFTY CLASSIC WALKS IN THE PENNINES – Terry Marsh *(£8.95)*
EAST CHESHIRE WALKS – Graham Beech *(£5.95)*
RAMBLES AROUND MANCHESTER – Mike Cresswell *(£5.95)*
YORKSHIRE DALES WALKING: On The Level – Norman Buckley *(£6.95)*
WALKS IN MYSTERIOUS WALES – Laurence Main *(£7.95)*
CHALLENGING WALKS: NW England & N Wales – Ron Astley (£7.95)
BEST PUB WALKS – CHESTER & THE DEE VALLEY – John Haywood *(£6.95)*
BEST PUB WALKS IN GWENT – Les Lumsdon *(£6.95)*
BEST PUB WALKS IN POWYS – Les Lumsdon & Chris Rushton *(£6.95)*
BEST PUB WALKS IN PEMBROKESHIRE – Laurence Main *(£6.95)*
BEST PUB WALKS IN THE NORTH PENNINES – Nick Channer (£6.95)

There are many more titles in our fabulous series of 'Best Pub Walks' books for just about every popular walking area in the UK, all featuring access by public transport. All of our books are available from your local bookshop. In case of difficulty, or to obtain our complete catalogue, please contact:

SIGMA LEISURE, 1 SOUTH OAK LANE, WILMSLOW, CHESHIRE SK9 6AR
Phone: 01625 – 531035   Fax: 01625 – 536800

ACCESS and VISA orders welcome – call our friendly sales staff or use our 24 hour Answer-phone service! Most orders are despatched on the day we receive your order – you could be enjoying our books in just a couple of days. Please add £2 p&p to all orders.